Oxford International Primary History

4

Pat Lunt

Oxford International Primary for enquiring minds

ASPIRE SUCCEED PROGRESS

OXFORD

Great Clarendon Street, Oxford, OX2 6DP, United Kingdom

Oxford University Press is a department of the University of Oxford. It furthers the University's objective of excellence in research, scholarship, and education by publishing worldwide. Oxford is a registered trade mark of Oxford University Press in the UK and in certain other countries.

© Pat Lunt 2017

The moral rights of the author have been asserted.

First published in 2017

All rights reserved. No part of this publication may be reproduced, stored in a retrieval system, or transmitted, in any form or by any means, without the prior permission in writing of Oxford University Press, or as expressly permitted by law, by licence or under terms agreed with the appropriate reprographics rights organization. Enquiries concerning reproduction outside the scope of the above should be sent to the Rights Department, Oxford University Press, at the address above.

You must not circulate this work in any other form and you must impose this same condition on any acquirer.

British Library Cataloguing in Publication Data
Data available

ISBN 978-0-19-841812-2

15

Paper used in the production of this book is a natural, recyclable product made from wood grown in sustainable forests. The manufacturing process conforms to the environmental regulations of the country of origin.

Printed in India by Multivista Global Pvt. Ltd.

Acknowledgements

Cover illustration: Carlos Molinari/Advocate Art

Artwork: Aptara

Photos: p4/5: Michele Burgess/Alamy; **p8:** Everett Collection Historical/Alamy; **p12 (L):** The Print Collector/Alamy; **p12 (R):** mark phillips/Alamy; **p14 (T):** age fotostock/Alamy; **p14 (B):** dpa picture alliance/Alamy; **p15 (T):** Lebrecht Music and Arts Photo Library/Alamy; **p15 (B):** Loop Images Ltd/Alamy; **p17:** The Print Collector/Alamy; **p18/19:** Schickert., Peter/Alamy; **p20:** funkyfood London - Paul Williams/Alamy; **p21:** Nicholas Dowling/Alamy; **p22:** Marshall Ikonography/Alamy; **p5, p19, p27, p30 & p33:** Michael Rosskothen/Shutterstock; **p28:** Attic red-figure cup depicting a rider on horseback (ceramic), Euphronios, (fl.c.520-500 BC) (workshop of)/Louvre, Paris, France/Bridgeman Images; **p29:** IORDANIS PALLIKARAS/Alamy; **p31:** PSL Images/Alamy; **p31/33:** Alistair Laming/Alamy; **p36:** REDA &CO srl/Alamy; **p38 (T):** AlgolOnline/Alamy; **p38 (B) & p61 (T):** Sean Pavone/Alamy; **p42 (T) & p61 (B):** Hemis/Alamy; **p42 (B):** Heritage Image Partnership Ltd/Alamy; **p43:** Rose-Marie Murray/Alamy; **p45:** steve estvanik/Shutterstock; **p46/47:** Konstantin Kalishko/Alamy; **p48:** PRISMA ARCHIVO/Alamy; **p49 (TR) & p58:** UniversalImagesGroup/Getty; **p49 (ML):** Oleksandr Rupeta / Alamy; **p49 (BR):** Jochen Tack/Alamy; **p50 (T):** Nick Pavlakis/Shutterstock; **p50 (B) & p59:** robertharding/Alamy; **p52:** The Great Wall of China, 1886 (w/c), Simpson, William 'Crimea' (1823-99)/Private Collection/Photo © Bonhams, London, UK/Bridgeman Images; **p53:** Hemis/Alamy; **p54:** charles best/Alamy; **p55:** Heritage Image Partnership Ltd/Alamy; **p56:** Photo 12/Alamy; **p57 (T):** Martin Leitch/Alamy; **p57 (B):** Chad Case/Alamy;

Although we have made every effort to trace and contact all copyright holders before publication this has not been possible in all cases. If notified, the publisher will rectify any errors or omissions at the earliest opportunity.

Links to third party websites are provided by Oxford in good faith and for information only. Oxford disclaims any responsibility for the materials contained in any third party website referenced in this work.

The manufacturer's authorised representative in the EU for product safety is Oxford University Press España S.A. of El Parque Empresarial San Fernando de Henares, Avenida de Castilla, 2 – 28830 Madrid (www.oup.es/en or product.safety@oup.com).
OUP España S.A. also acts as importer into Spain of products made by the manufacturer.

Contents

1 Ancient Egypt

- 1.1 Egypt and the pharaohs — 6
- 1.2 Farming and trade — 8
- 1.3 Everyday life in Ancient Egypt — 10
- 1.4 Tombs and treasures — 12
- 1.5 The Egyptian influence – evidence and inspiration — 14
- 1 Review — 16

2 Ancient Greece

- 2.1 Who were the Ancient Greeks? — 20
- 2.2 Work and relaxation in Ancient Greece — 22
- 2.3 Everyday life in Ancient Greece — 24
- 2.4 Soldiers and seafarers — 26
- 2.5 Trade, art and ideas — 28
- 2 Review — 30

3 Ancient Rome

- 3.1 The beginnings of Ancient Rome — 34
- 3.2 The Roman Empire begins — 36
- 3.3 Ancient Roman towns and cities — 38
- 3.4 Everyday life in the Roman empire — 40
- 3.5 Art and culture of Ancient Rome — 42
- 3 Review — 44

4 A history of leisure and recreation

- 4.1 Games — 48
- 4.2 Sport — 50
- 4.3 Have people always gone on holiday? — 52
- 4.4 Storytelling as entertainment — 54
- 4.5 Educational recreation — 56
- 4 Review — 58

Vocabulary quiz — 60
Glossary — 62

1 Ancient Egypt

In this unit you will:
- explain the importance of the River Nile in Ancient Egypt
- analyse the structure of Ancient Egyptian society
- assess daily life and work in Ancient Egypt
- identify types of historical evidence for life in Ancient Egypt
- consider the influence of the Ancient Egyptians on other civilisations

Egyptologist sarcophagus pyramid dynasty hieroglyphics

❓ Look at the photo on this page. How do you think the pyramids were built? Who do you think ordered them to be built? What do you think they were for?

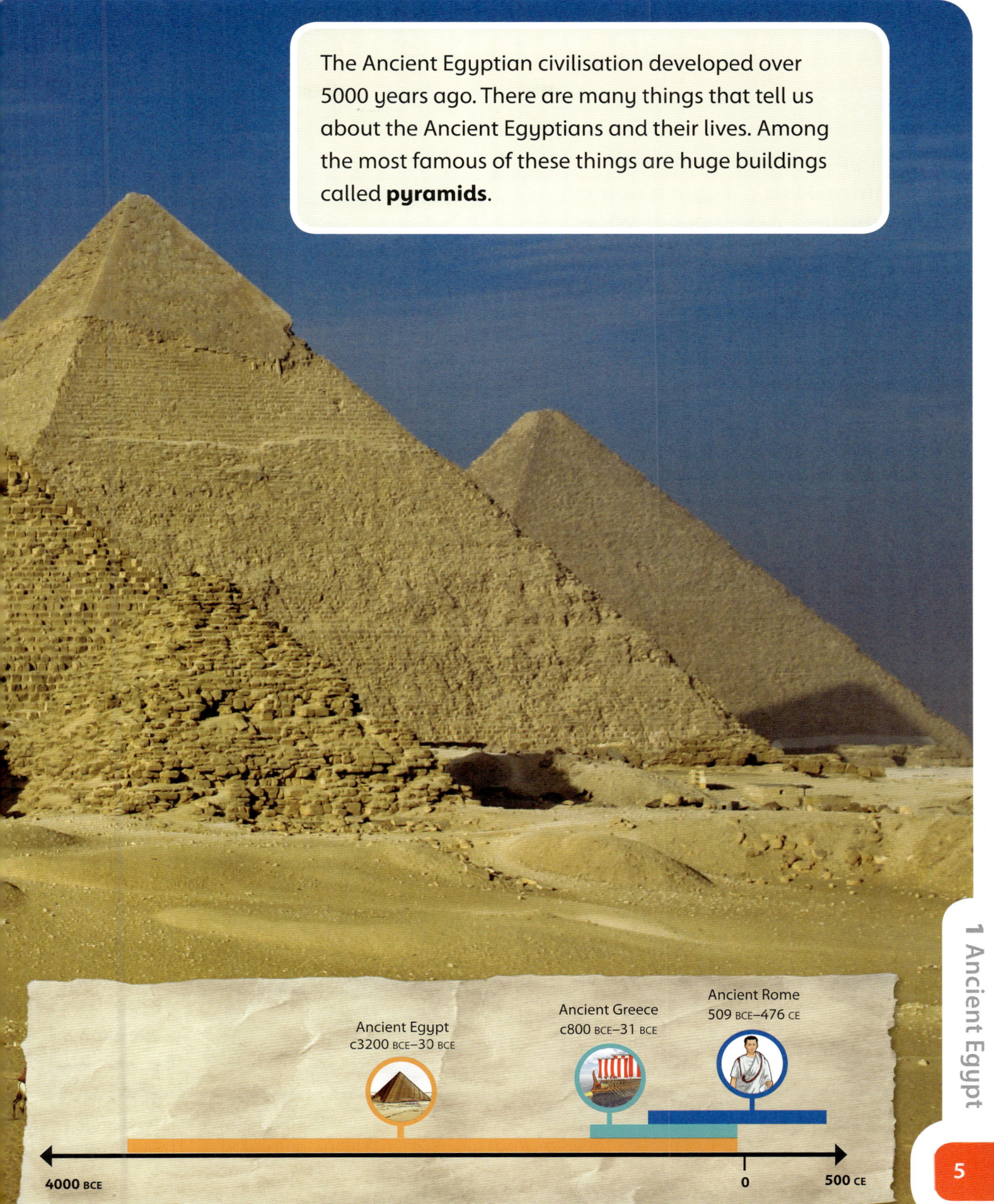

The Ancient Egyptian civilisation developed over 5000 years ago. There are many things that tell us about the Ancient Egyptians and their lives. Among the most famous of these things are huge buildings called **pyramids**.

Ancient Egypt c3200 BCE–30 BCE

Ancient Greece c800 BCE–31 BCE

Ancient Rome 509 BCE–476 CE

4000 BCE — 0 — 500 CE

1.1 Egypt and the pharaohs

Egypt is a country in North Africa. Most of Egypt is desert with little or no rainfall. What made it possible for the Ancient Egyptian civilisation to develop here? Who were the rulers of this powerful kingdom? Why did the civilisation end?

Egypt and the River Nile

Egypt is in North Africa. To the east is the Red Sea and to the north is the Mediterranean Sea.

The River Nile flows north for 7000 kilometres through several African countries. It flows through the whole of Egypt.

In ancient times, the Nile usually flooded each year. When the water moved back it left behind a thick layer of mud. The mud made the surrounding lands very fertile. The Ancient Egyptians could usually grow more than enough food to feed everybody in the area.

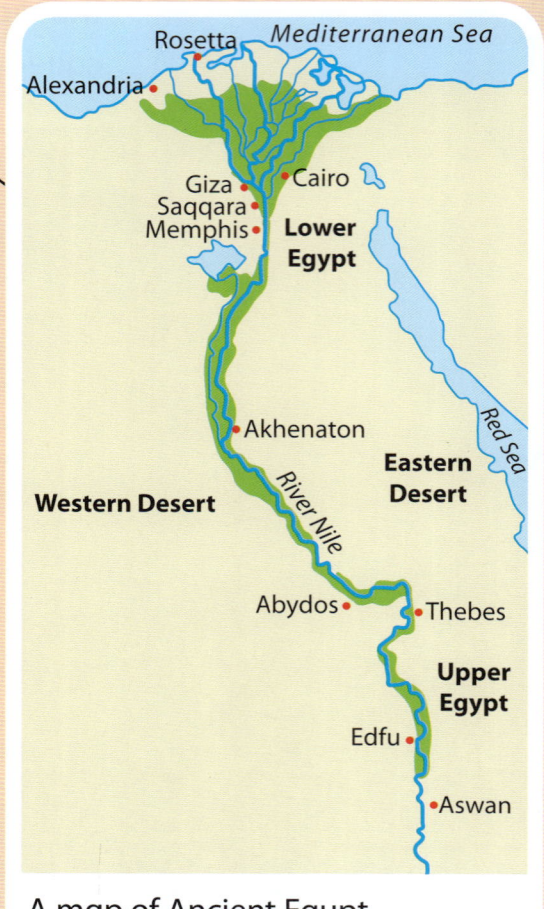

A map of Ancient Egypt

2650 BCE First step pyramid built by Djoser

3100 BCE King Narmer united the two kingdoms of Egypt

2580–2560 BCE Great pyramid built at Giza

1630–1523 BCE The Hyksos people invaded

1332 BCE Tutankhamun came to power

3200 BCE

Old Kingdom (2570–2130 BCE)

Middle Kingdom (1940–1600 BCE)

New Kingdom (1540–1070 BCE)

Some important events from the history of Ancient Egypt

Who were the pharaohs?

The pharaohs were the kings or queens of Ancient Egypt. The pharaoh owned all the land. The pharaoh made the laws and received taxes from the people.

Over 170 pharaohs ruled Egypt. There were 30 different **dynasties**, which are families of rulers.

Why do we remember different pharaohs?

We know about the pharaohs because the Ancient Egyptian people wrote down the things that the pharaohs did. People made pictures showing events from the pharaohs' lives, carved into rock or painted onto walls. We remember some pharaohs because they ordered huge structures to be built. We remember other pharaohs because they were powerful warriors. Some pharaohs are famous because they were women, at a time when most powerful people were men.

The most famous pharaoh is probably Tutankhamun. He was not actually a very important pharaoh. We remember him because his tomb contained many treasures.

Activities

1. Work with a friend. Discuss and write down your answers.
   a. Why do you think most Ancient Egyptian settlements were near the River Nile?
   b. How did a good supply of food help the Egyptian civilisation to develop?
2. Work in a group. Make a display showing a timeline of some of the important pharaohs of Ancient Egypt.

Challenge

A historian from Ancient Greece who lived in the 5th century BCE said Egypt was 'The gift of the Nile'. What do you think he meant? Do you think this is a good description?

332 BCE
Alexander the Great invaded

30 BCE
Cleopatra, the last Greek pharaoh, died

Late Period (650–320 BCE)

Ptolemaic Dynasty (320–30 BCE)

Glossary words

fertile   tax

1.2 Farming and trade

The River Nile made it possible for farmers to grow crops. Which crops did they grow and what did they use the crops for? The Ancient Egyptians also traded with other people. What did they trade and who were their trading partners?

Farming and the Nile

Fertile soil near the River Nile helped farmers grow crops. Farmers dug channels from the river to the fields to water the crops. They used a shaduf to lift water from the channels onto the fields.

Which crops did farmers produce?

Farmers grew cereals such as wheat and barley. They grew vegetables, including onions, beans and cucumbers. They grew fruit such as melons, pomegranates and grapes. Farmers had to give part of their produce, especially grain, to the **government** as tax.

Did Ancient Egyptian farmers keep animals?

Working farm animals included oxen and donkeys. Cows and goats provided milk. Ducks and geese provided meat and eggs.

What was trade in Ancient Egypt like?

The Egyptians traded grain, gold, papyrus, pottery and dates. They imported other goods, including: metals, wood for buildings and furniture, gem stones, incense, myrrh and oils.

Merchants used boats to transport goods along the River Nile, across the Red Sea and around the Mediterranean Sea. They transported some goods over land.

Early merchant boats were made of reeds. Later boats were built from wood.

Glossary words

government	myrrh
import	papyrus
incense	shaduf

A Oxen pulled ploughs.

B The River Nile was used for transporting goods.

C People used nets and hunting sticks to catch water birds such as ducks.

D Grain was thrown up in the air. The wind blew away the light, empty husks. Clean grain fell back down.

E Oxen walked over harvested crops. They separated the grain from the outer husk.

F Grain was stored away from mice and rats.

G A shaduf

H People caught fish using spears and nets.

Activities

1 Write a report on Ancient Egyptian farming. Use the picture on this page to help you describe what work people did. Try to imagine the smells and sounds to make your report more interesting.

2 Research and write about the goods that the Ancient Egyptians traded. Explain what the goods were used for.

Challenge

Use books and the Internet to find out about the three seasons of the Ancient Egyptian year: Akhet, Peret and Shemu. Prepare a presentation with illustrations to explain: when the seasons were; what happened during each season; what people did during each season.

1.3 Everyday life in Ancient Egypt

The Ancient Egyptian pharaohs, and people in the royal palaces, lived a life of luxury. What was life like for the rest of the people? What work did people do and what were their homes like? What food did they eat?

What different types of work did people have?

The society in Ancient Egypt was organised as a hierarchy. A person's job marked that person's place in society.

Glossary words

hierarchy
society
stonemason

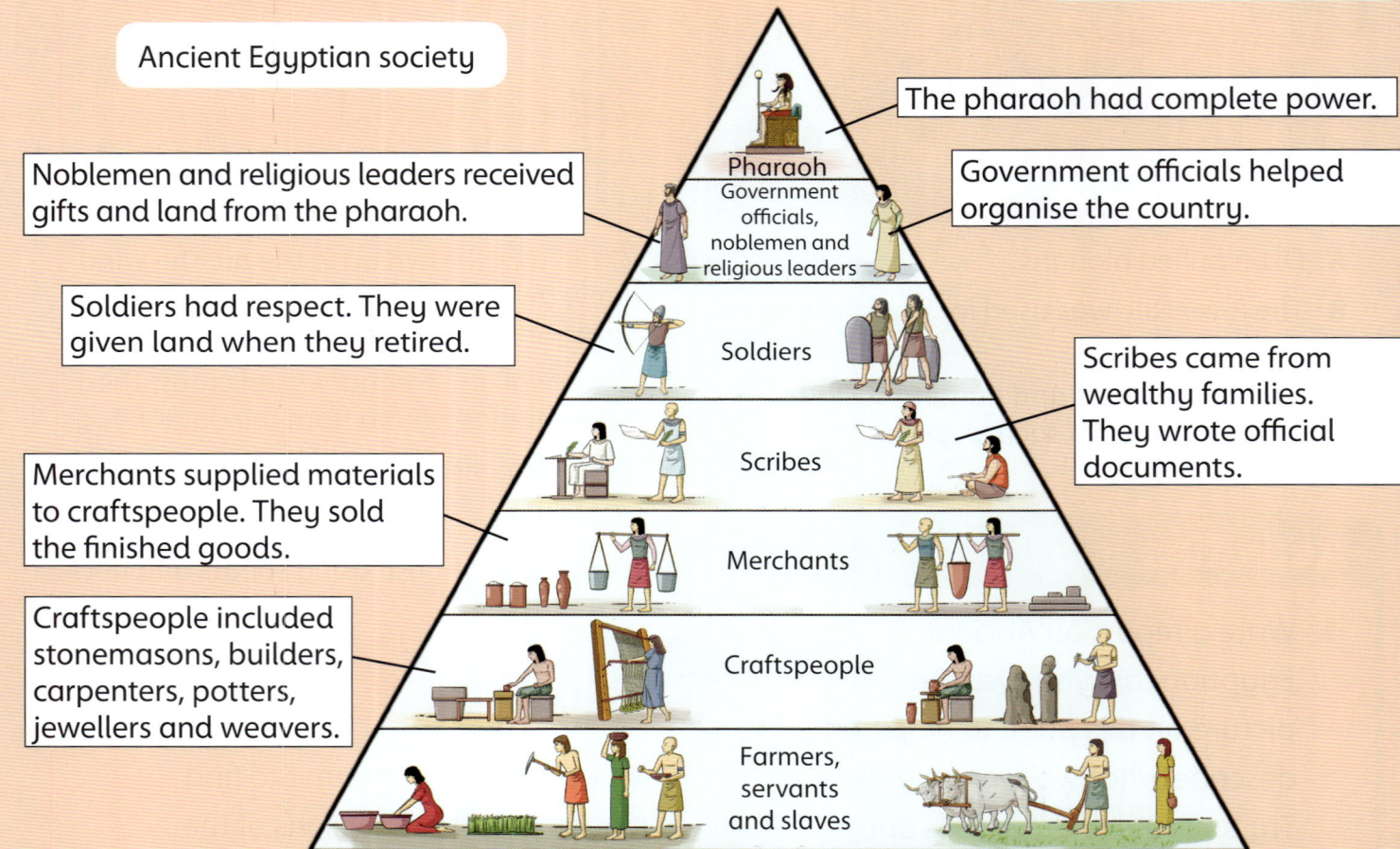

Ancient Egyptian society

- The pharaoh had complete power.
- Noblemen and religious leaders received gifts and land from the pharaoh.
- Government officials helped organise the country.
- Soldiers had respect. They were given land when they retired.
- Scribes came from wealthy families. They wrote official documents.
- Merchants supplied materials to craftspeople. They sold the finished goods.
- Craftspeople included stonemasons, builders, carpenters, potters, jewellers and weavers.
- Most people worked as peasant farmers on other people's land.
- Servants worked for other people and were paid.
- Slaves were captured prisoners or people from very poor families.

Pyramid levels (top to bottom): Pharaoh; Government officials, noblemen and religious leaders; Soldiers; Scribes; Merchants; Craftspeople; Farmers, servants and slaves.

What did ordinary people wear?

People wore light linen clothing. Linen is made from the fibres of the flax plant. The light clothes kept people cool and protected them from the hot sun.

What were Ancient Egyptian houses like?

Towns and villages were built on higher ground to be safe from flooding.

Be a good historian

A good historian wants to make connections and find contrasts. You can do this too. Compare the organisation of Ancient Egyptian society with societies from different periods and places.

- The reed roof provided shade to keep cool.
- Clothes and sheets dried in the sun.
- People used the flat roof for eating and sleeping.
- Houses were built with bricks of mud and straw.
- The small, high windows kept the house cool.
- Inside there was a family room with little furniture.
- Grains were stored for making bread.
- Bedroom
- The food prepared in the kitchen was mainly bread, fruit and vegetables.
- Storage
- Animals were kept in the enclosed yard: goats for milk and geese for eggs. People hardly ever ate meat.

An Egyptian worker's home

Activities

1. Work in a group. Research the work of a craftsperson in Ancient Egypt. Prepare a presentation for the class.
2. Discuss how life for craftspeople, farmers and servants was different from life for scribes, government officials and nobles.

Challenge

Find out about one of the cities of Ancient Egypt. Where was it? Who built it? How many people lived there?

1.4 Tombs and treasures

Ancient Egypt is famous for buildings known as pyramids. The pharaohs ordered the pyramids to be build. What were these buildings for? Where and how were they built? What did they contain?

The pyramids

The Ancient Egyptians believed that when people died they went to live another life in another place. The bodies of rich Egyptians were prepared for the next life in a special way. The body was preserved in a process called mummification. The preserved body is called a mummy.

The mummy was placed inside a decorated coffin called a **sarcophagus**.

Pharaohs were buried with many treasures. The pyramid was a special tomb. Pyramids were built to protect the preserved body and the treasures. Pyramids were a symbol of power and wealth.

Passageways inside the pyramid were designed to confuse tomb robbers.

Burial chamber

Items of treasure were buried with the pharaoh deep inside the pyramid.

This is the head of the sarcophagus of Lady Henutmehyt. She lived from 1279 to 1213 BCE.

Where were the pyramids built?

Boats transported the huge blocks used to build the pyramids up the River Nile. Most pyramids were built near the river so that the workers did not have to move the blocks far.

Did you know?

The pyramids have angled sides that represent the rays of the sun.

How were the pyramids built?

No-one is completely sure how the pyramids were built. We know some things from writing, drawings, tools and objects that have been found. The builders had to achieve many things. They had to: make a huge level area for the base of the pyramid; organise the workers who cut and moved millions of stone blocks; make sure the sides of the pyramid were built at the correct angle so that the pyramid did not collapse.

The largest and most famous pyramid is the Great Pyramid of Khufu. This pyramid was built using more than 2 million huge stone blocks. The whole structure was covered in limestone blocks to give a smooth, white surface that shone in the sun.

Where were later pharaohs buried?

The Egyptians used the pyramids for their royal tombs until about 1540 BCE. After this date, the pharaohs were buried in the Valley of the Kings. This valley is on the west bank of the Nile, opposite Thebes.

Tomb robbers stole everything from most of the tombs in both the pyramids and the Valley of the Kings.

Glossary words

preserve   tomb

Why do we remember Pharaoh Tutankhamun?

Tutankhamun was a pharaoh who ruled Egypt from 1332 to 1323 BCE. Tutankhamun was not a very important pharaoh in his time. Yet he is probably the most famous pharaoh today.

He was buried in the Valley of the Kings. His tomb was not disturbed for over 3000 years. In 1922, an **Egyptologist** called Howard Carter discovered the tomb. Tutankhamun's tomb was well preserved. It contained hundreds of objects that have helped historians build up a picture of life in Ancient Egypt.

Activities

1. Pyramids were very expensive to build. Discuss with a partner why the pharaohs wanted to create these huge buildings.
2. Use books and the Internet to research the different stages of building a pyramid. Make a class display to show your findings.

Challenge

Use books and the Internet to research ancient archeological sites in your country. Write a fact sheet describing where the sites are, how old they are and what was found there.

1.5 The Egyptian influence – evidence and inspiration

Examples of Egyptian art and writing have survived for thousands of years. What do they tell us about life in Ancient Egypt? What ideas did the Ancient Egyptians pass on to other people at the time? What influence has Egyptian art had in modern times?

How did the Egyptians influence other written languages?

The Ancient Egyptians developed a kind of writing called **hieroglyphics**. This writing used pictures to represent different words, sounds, objects, actions and ideas.

Writing changed over the time of the Egyptian civilisation. The Egyptians created forms of writing that were easier and faster to write. People from different countries used and changed the hieroglyphics. Alphabets used around the world today have developed from Egyptian hieroglyphics.

Hieroglyphic writing from the tomb of Queen Nefertari in Luxor, Egypt

How can we read Egyptian hieroglyphics?

In 1799, a block of stone was discovered near the Egyptian port of Rosetta (now Rashid). The stone was carved with the same text in three different languages. One language was Ancient Greek, which many scholars could read. After 20 years of study, Frenchman Jean-François Champollion produced the first translation of hieroglyphics.

The Rosetta Stone helped people to understand Ancient Egyptian hieroglyphics.

Glossary words

architecture   culture   evidence

Paintings and carvings

Ancient Egyptian wall paintings and carvings tell us about the pharaohs and many parts of everyday life. They help us find out about Ancient Egyptian food, clothing, work and recreation.

Art as inspiration

Merchants and travellers took ideas from Ancient Egypt to other countries. We can see Egyptian ideas in the art and architecture of Ancient Greece and of 17th- and 18th-century Europe.

The discovery of Tutankhamun's tomb in 1922 created huge interest in Ancient Egyptian art, culture and heritage. Egyptian art influenced architecture, design and art for many years.

Egyptian mathematics

The Egyptians used measurements based on body parts such as the width of the palm of a hand. By about 2700 BCE, they had developed a number system based on 10. They knew about prime numbers, unit fractions and geometry.

Many ideas we have about mathematics today can be traced back to the Ancient Egyptians.

In this picture a scribe is inspecting a flock of geese. Can you see the different objects he is using? What do you think his clothes are made of?

The Egyptian influence is clear to see in this factory built in 1926–1928 in London, England.

Did you know?

The Egyptians developed a calendar with 12 months of 30 days and with 5 extra feast days.

Activities

1. Write an explanation of how wall paintings help us understand parts of life in Ancient Egypt.
2. In a group, research three buildings that were inspired by Egyptian architecture. Write about each building, including where it is.

Challenge

Write a brief explanation of why you think we remember the Ancient Egyptians.

1 Review

Answer these questions in your notebook.

Choose the best answer from the choices below. Write a, b or c as your answer.

1. Egypt is on the continent of:
   a. Asia
   b. Africa
   c. Europe
2. In Ancient Egypt, the power of a pharaoh usually passed to a member of the same family. Families who rule in this way are called:
   a. heirlooms
   b. corporations
   c. dynasties
3. The main reason why Egyptian farmers were able to grow lots of different crops was:
   a. the soil near the River Nile was very fertile
   b. the warm climate helped crops to grow
   c. the soil in Ancient Egypt was very soft
4. The Egyptians needed to trade for some of the goods they needed. One material that they needed to import for building and furniture was:
   a. copper
   b. stone
   c. wood
5. Some people had the important job of reading and writing documents. These people were called:
   a. viziers
   b. scribes
   c. merchants
6. Most Ancient Egyptians wore light clothing made from:
   a. linen
   b. cotton
   c. wool
7. The name of the pharaoh who ordered the first Egyptian pyramid to be built was:
   a. Khufu
   b. Tutankhamun
   c. Djoser
8. Early Ancient Egyptian writing is called:
   a. neoglyphics
   b. hieroglyphics
   c. dieroglyphics

Read these statements and decide if they are true or false. Write 'True' or 'False' for each one.

9. The Ancient Egyptian civilisation lasted for more than 5000 years.
10. The Great Pyramid of Khufu was built using about 2000 stone blocks.

Now use this map to complete these tasks.

11 In your notebook, write the names of the six cities shown. The first letter of each city is given to help you.

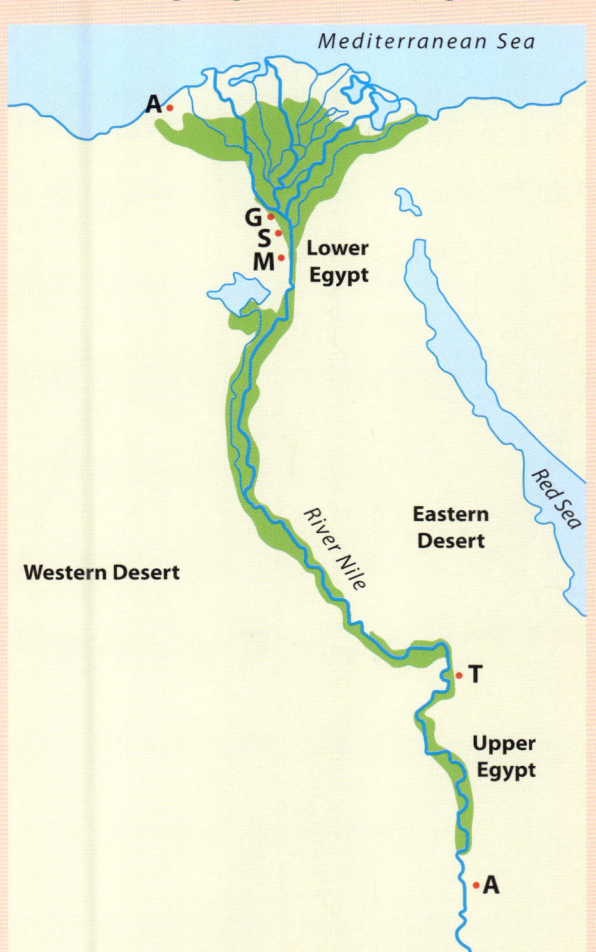

12 Describe where the Ancient Egyptian merchant boats travelled. Use the map to help you.

Now complete these tasks.

13 'Life in Ancient Egypt was good for everyone.' Do you agree or disagree with this statement? Write a short essay to explain your answer.

14 Imagine you are a craftsperson in Ancient Egypt. Choose a craft and write about your work. Describe:
- the objects you make
- the tools you use
- the materials you need
- where you get your materials
- who buys and uses the things you make.

15 Imagine you have discovered this wall painting in the tomb of an Ancient Egyptian nobleman. Write a description of the painting. Describe what the painting shows and what it tells us about Ancient Egyptian:
- clothes
- hairstyles
- plants
- animals
- food
- hunting
- transport.

2 Ancient Greece

In this unit you will:
- explore who the Ancient Greeks were
- analyse and describe everyday life in Ancient Greece
- describe how the Greeks fought wars on land and at sea
- consider the influence of the Ancient Greeks on other civilisations

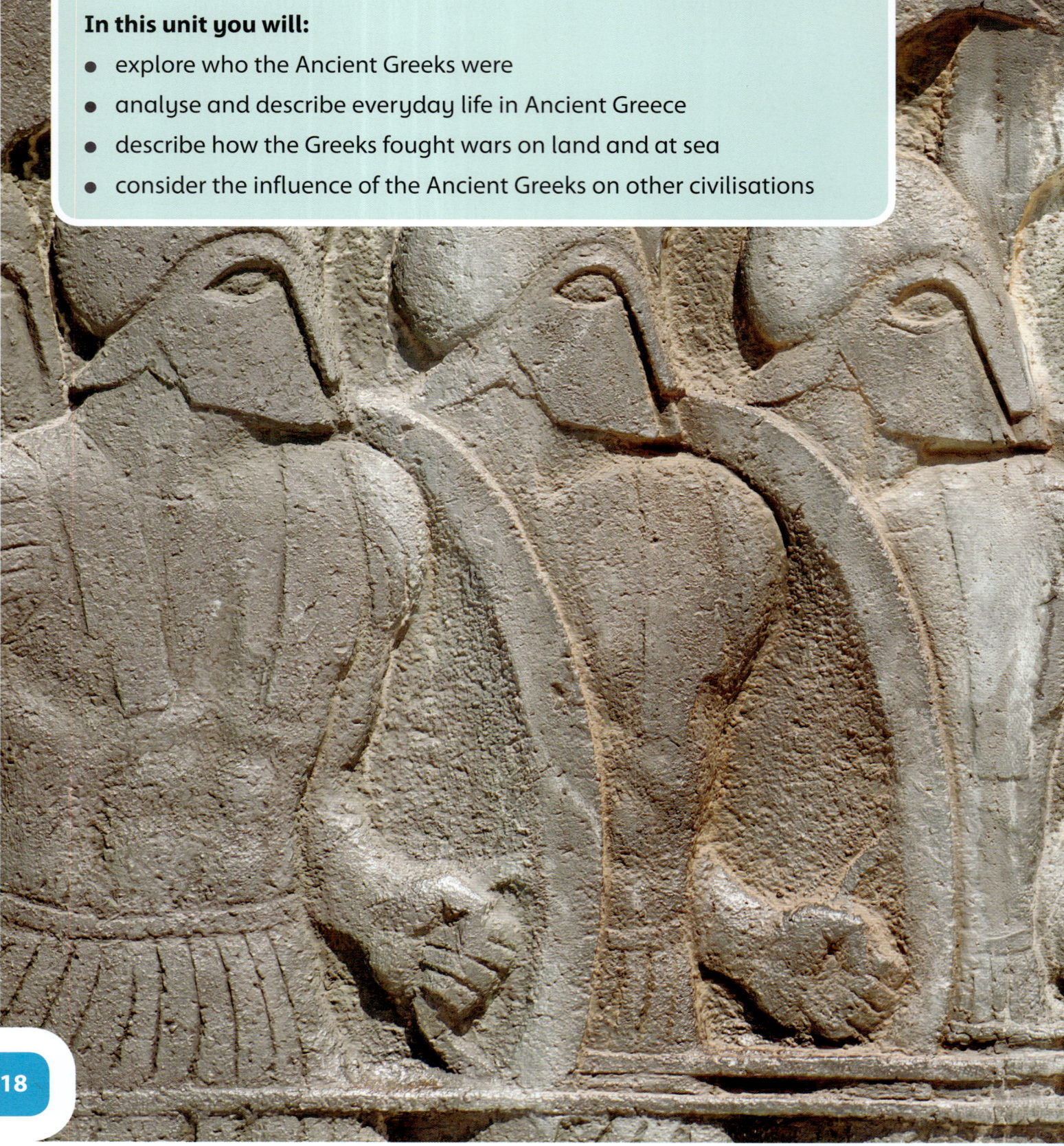

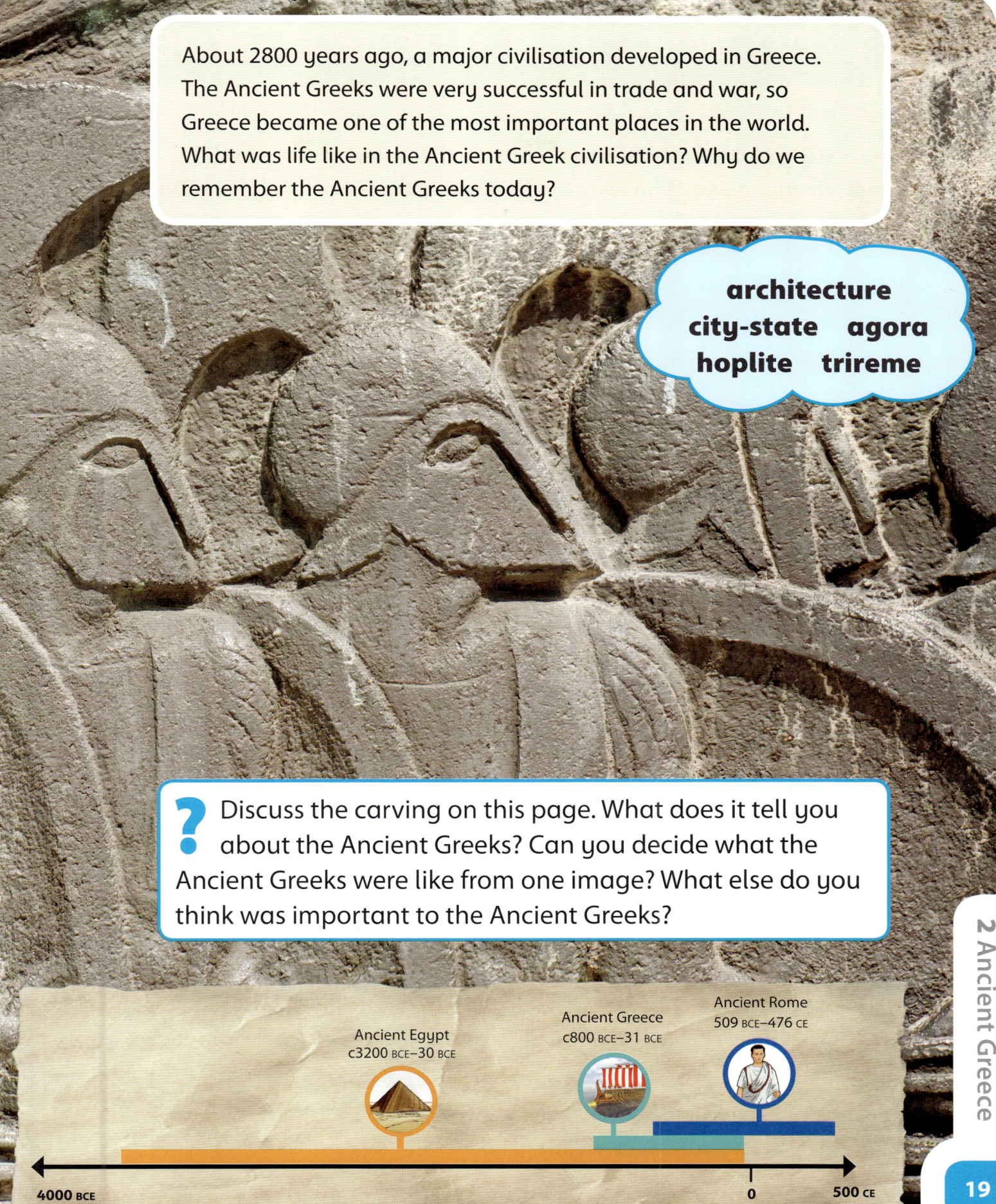

About 2800 years ago, a major civilisation developed in Greece. The Ancient Greeks were very successful in trade and war, so Greece became one of the most important places in the world. What was life like in the Ancient Greek civilisation? Why do we remember the Ancient Greeks today?

**architecture
city-state   agora
hoplite   trireme**

? Discuss the carving on this page. What does it tell you about the Ancient Greeks? Can you decide what the Ancient Greeks were like from one image? What else do you think was important to the Ancient Greeks?

Ancient Egypt
c3200 BCE–30 BCE

Ancient Greece
c800 BCE–31 BCE

Ancient Rome
509 BCE–476 CE

4000 BCE   0   500 CE

2 Ancient Greece

2.1 Who were the Ancient Greeks?

The history of Greek civilisation starts on the island of Crete in the Mediterranean Sea. Who were the inhabitants of this island? How did Greek civilisations change? How was society organised and who were the rulers?

Early Greek civilisations

The Minoans developed the first Greek civilisation. This civilisation began on the island of Crete. It lasted from about 2700 BCE until about 1450 BCE. Then another civilisation began on mainland Greece. This was the Mycenaean civilisation, which lasted until about 1100 BCE.

We do not know what happened for the next 300 years because there is no writing or art from this time.

The largest Minoan settlement on Crete was at Knossos.

The Archaic Period

The time from about 750 BCE to about 480 BCE is known as the Archaic Period. The population of Greece increased and the Greeks traded more with other countries. The Greek people began to use written language again.

The people lived in **city-states**. Each city and its surrounding territory formed a separate state with its own government. Each city-state also had its own calendar, laws and army.

Most city-states were ruled by a small group of powerful people or a single tyrant. In about 510 BCE, the people of Athens developed a new idea. They decided that the men of the city should meet to decide how to manage the city. This type of government is called a democracy. The city of Athens no longer had just one ruler.

The city-states often fought each other. City-states joined forces in wars against the Persian Empire between 492 and 449 BCE.

Glossary words

culture
democracy
government
philosophy
tyrant

Classical Greece

The Classical Greek period began in about 480 BCE. There were great advances in science, philosophy, mathematics, art, literature and **architecture**.

Philip of Macedon took control of all the city-states in 338 BCE. His son, Alexander the Great, created a Greek empire that reached across Egypt, Asia Minor and into India. Ideas from Greek culture spread to all these places.

Hellenistic Greece

After Alexander's death in 323 BCE, his generals divided the empire between them. Greece became part of the Roman Empire in 31 BCE.

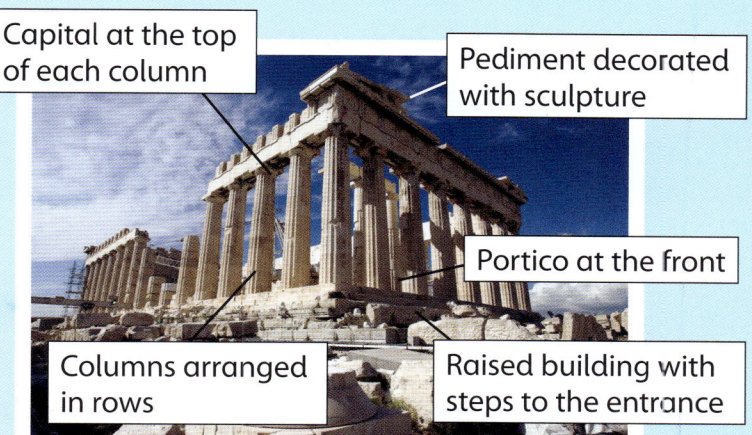

Ruins of the Parthenon in Athens, built between 447 and 438 BCE.

- Capital at the top of each column
- Pediment decorated with sculpture
- Portico at the front
- Columns arranged in rows
- Raised building with steps to the entrance

Did you know?

Alexander the Great founded at least 20 cities called Alexandria.

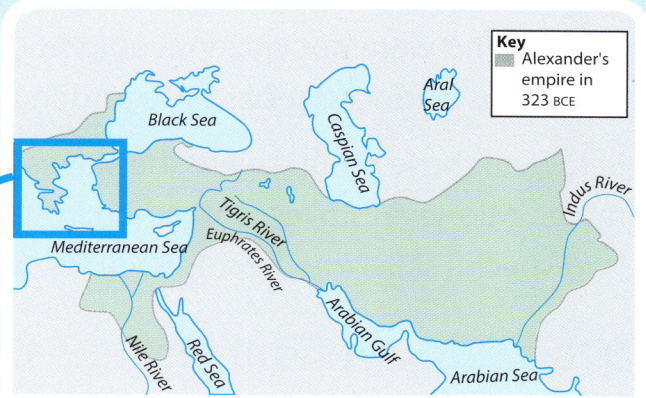

Alexander the Great expanded the empire from 336 BCE.

People moved to lands around the Aegean Sea from about 750 BCE to find new farmland.

Challenge

Find out about the climate and landscape in Greece. What challenges did Ancient Greek farmers have?

Activities

1. Draw a timeline showing the main stages in the history of Greek civilisations.

2. Work in a group. Carry out research on one of the city-states on the map. Find out some interesting facts about your chosen city-state.

2.2 Work and relaxation in Ancient Greece

Many Ancient Greeks lived in the city within a city-state. Many more lived in the countryside. The work that people did depended on their rank in society. What did people do when they were not working?

What work did different people do?

The most important group in Greek society was the citizens. High-ranking citizens were rich. They owned land and property. Middle-ranking citizens often owned small farms or worked as fishermen. Citizens also worked in government and as teachers, scientists, doctors and artists. The lowest-ranking citizens worked as craftsmen, merchants and soldiers.

People who were not citizens could not own property. They worked for wealthier citizens as cleaners, cooks and gardeners.

Below all these groups were the slaves. Low-ranking slaves worked in quarries or mines. Mid-level slaves worked on farms or in wealthy households. Some slaves had special skills and became nurses, teachers or craftspeople.

What did Ancient Greeks do in their free time?

Rich Ancient Greeks used their free time for improving their minds. Men enjoyed discussing politics, religion and philosophy. Men and boys also kept fit at the public gymnasium.

The Ancient Greeks loved theatre. The plays were either tragedies or comedies. The actors, who were all men, wore masks when they acted as different characters.

Theatres were decorated with carvings of theatrical masks.

Glossary words

comedy   politics   tragedy   citizen

Women and slaves visited the **agora**. They bought goods for the household and heard the latest news.

The Ancient Greeks loved sports. Most cities had a stadium where people could watch running races. There were also several national sporting events. The most important sporting event was the Olympic Games.

The main market and meeting place in the city was called the agora.

What did children do for fun?

Greek children played with dolls made from pottery, wood or rags. They also had rattles, hoops and balls made from rags tied together. They played a game called knucklebones using real sheep bones.

Greek children had a range of toys to play with. Do you play with any similar toys?

Activities

1. Draw a diagram that explains the structure of society in Ancient Greece. Use the information on this page to help you.
2. Find out and write about the game of knucklebones and about any modern games that have developed from knucklebones.

Did you know?

The first Olympic Games were held in 776 BCE. Every four years, athletes from different city-states competed against each other. About 50 000 people attended from different parts of the Greek world.

Challenge

Find out and write about the four sporting festivals of Ancient Greece.

2.3 Everyday life in Ancient Greece

Family life in Ancient Greece was centred around the home. Life was different for men and women. What roles and responsibilities did different family members have? What did the children do?

What were Ancient Greek homes like?

Homes for most of the population were plain and simple. They were built from mud bricks on a stone foundation. Wooden beams supported a roof of overlapping clay tiles.

What was life like for men?

Men were in control of most parts of life in Ancient Greece, including the house. Men used part of the house called the andron to entertain friends and business contacts.

Homes of wealthy families were built around a courtyard so that cool air reached all the rooms.

What was life like for women?

Women had to stay in the house unless a man went out with them. Women who had no slaves did household chores and looked after children. Women cooked, span thread and wove cloth. Women had a special room called the gynaikon.

What was life like for children?

Boys from poorer families helped their fathers at work. Boys from richer families went to school from the age of 7. They learned to read and write and studied mathematics and history.

Girls did not go to school. They stayed at home and learned how to cook and do housework. Most girls married when they were between 13 and 16 years old.

In the city-state of Sparta, both boys and girls went to school. They had physical education to become strong and they learned to fight.

What did the Ancient Greeks eat?

Most people had a simple diet. Basic foods were porridge and bread made from barley. Most people did not eat meat often. Their food included fruit, vegetables, lentils, cheese, fish and beans. Olive oil was an important part of the diet.

What did the Ancient Greeks wear?

People wore a simple tunic called a chiton. Women or slaves made the clothes. Summer clothes were made of linen and winter clothes were made of wool. Rich people's clothing was dyed different colours.

In cold weather people wore a cloak called a himation.

A chiton was made of a single piece of cloth.

Pins held the chiton in place.

Children's clothes were similar to adults' clothes.

Women's clothes reached the ground.

People sometimes wore leather sandals.

Men's chitons were often knee length.

Most people were barefooted.

Activities

1 Imagine you are a child in Ancient Greece. Write to a child in another country. Describe a typical day and what you hope to do in the future.

2 Discuss in a group how household chores in an Ancient Greek house were different from chores today. Share your ideas with the class.

Glossary words

andron　　chores　　gynaikon

Challenge

Find out about the different types of homes in a city in Ancient Greece. What size were the houses? How many rooms did they have? What features were there?

2.4 Soldiers and seafarers

The Greek city-states were always arguing and often went to war with each other. Sometimes they joined together to fight a bigger enemy. Who could be a Greek soldier? How did Greek soldiers fight? What tactics did the Greeks use when fighting at sea?

Soldiers

An Ancient Greek army was made up mostly of foot-soldiers called **hoplites**. Hoplites were not professional soldiers. They were citizens who had to carry out military duties.

- Helmet often decorated with a crest of horse hair
- A richer man's helmet had cheek plates made of bronze
- Spear: 2.5–4.5 metres long
- Wooden shield with an outer layer of bronze
- Armour made of bronze for richer men, leather or layers of cloth for poorer men
- A hoplite only used his sword if his spear was lost or broken
- Metal armour to protect the shins
- Hoplites provided their own equipment. They carried food such as grains and cheese in a bag

Fighting formation

Hoplites fought side by side in lines. A group of 8–10 lines of soldiers was called a phalanx. The soldiers moved forwards together. Their shields formed a barrier. They held their spears under the arm pointing forwards. It was difficult for the enemy to break through the phalanx or to stop it.

Sometimes the phalanx was supported by cavalry and archers and by soldiers throwing stones.

War at sea

Ship design and construction were very advanced in Ancient Greece. The largest ships used in battles were called **triremes**. They had three rows of oars. The word is made from two Latin words: 'tri' meaning 'three' and 'remus' meaning 'oar'.

Glossary words

archer
cavalry

A rowing master shouted instructions for the oarsmen. A piper played a musical instrument called an aulos to help the oarsmen keep time.

The two main tactics were ramming and boarding. In battle, a ship's commander ordered the ship to steer straight at an enemy. When the ship struck, it smashed a hole in the wooden side of the enemy ship. The oarsmen of the Greek ship then rowed backwards in case the enemy ship started to sink.

The hoplites defended the ship. They sometimes boarded the enemy ship and fought to capture it.

The greatest sea battle in Greek history was fought against a Persian fleet near Salamis in 480 BCE. The battle was a great victory for the Greeks.

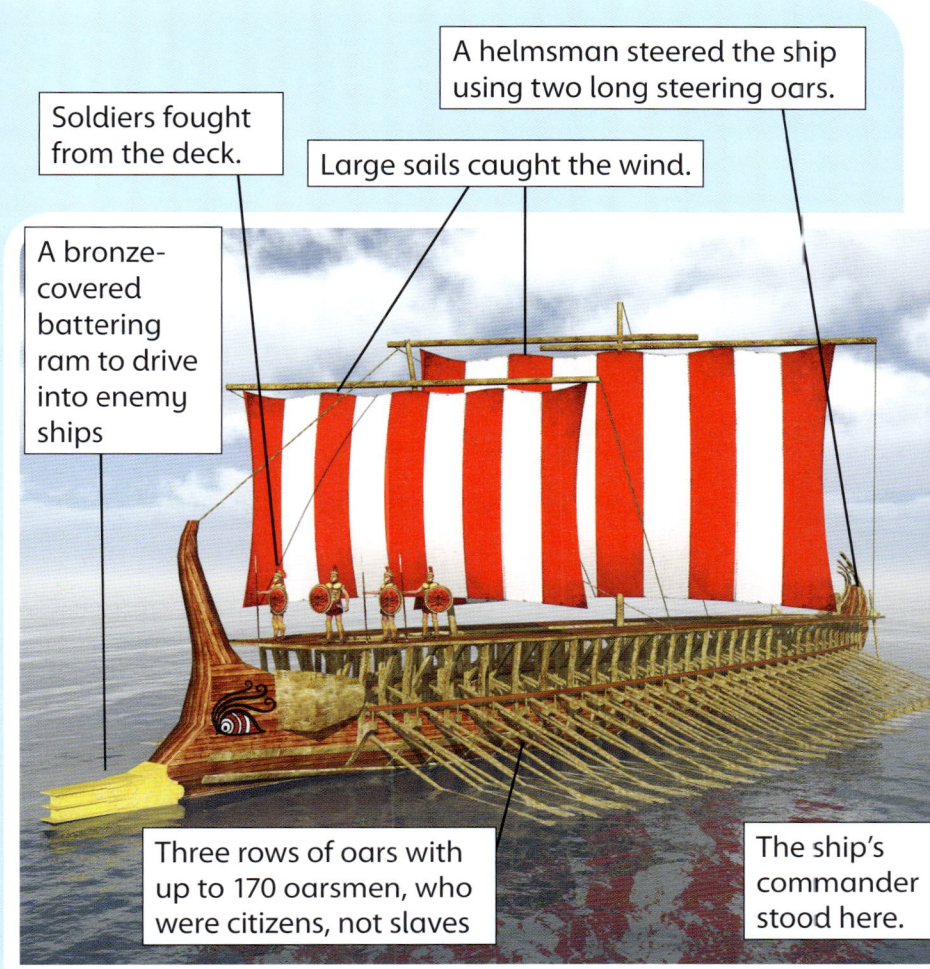

- A helmsman steered the ship using two long steering oars.
- Soldiers fought from the deck.
- Large sails caught the wind.
- A bronze-covered battering ram to drive into enemy ships
- Three rows of oars with up to 170 oarsmen, who were citizens, not slaves
- The ship's commander stood here.

A trireme

Did you know?

Greek soldiers sang as they marched to battle while musicians played pipes and trumpets. This helped the men to march in time and to feel confident and enthusiastic.

Activities

1. Make a poster ordering the men in an Ancient Greek city to report for military duty. The poster should describe what weapons, clothing and other items the men must provide.
2. Imagine you are a hoplite on a trireme. Write a report of a sea battle. Describe the tactics used in the battle.

Challenge

Use reference books and the Internet to research the Battle of Marathon, Thermopylae or Salamis. Write about 100 words to describe the battle.

2.5 Trade, art and ideas

Trade was important for the Ancient Greeks. They traded goods and also shared ideas, knowledge and techniques. Which countries traded with Greece and what influence did the Greeks have on other cultures?

Trade by sea

The Greeks used special trading boats to carry large loads over long distances. They set up trading posts in many places where merchants from different countries met to trade their goods.

Trade and art

Ordinary exports from Ancient Greece included wine, olives, olive oil, marble and pottery.

Ancient Greece traded these goods for glass, gold and silver. Greek craftspeople developed techniques to make jewellery.

Glossary words

architect, literature, exports, sculptor

Greek pottery was an important trade item and has been found in many places.

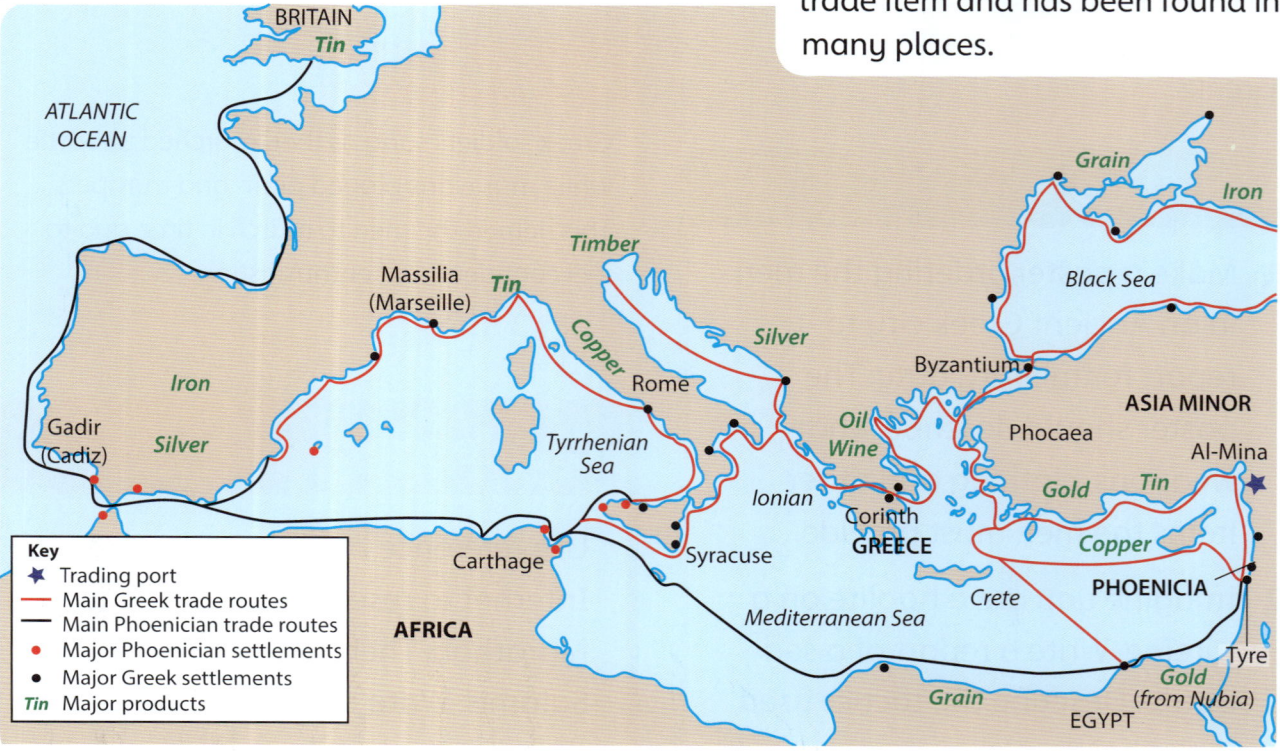

The Greeks and the Phoenicians controlled trade throughout the Mediterranean region.

Did you know?

The Egyptians admired Greek literature and had a library with at least 40 000 papyrus scrolls. Sadly, these were all lost when a Roman emperor burned the library down.

The Greeks became very skilled sculptors. They made figures of people and animals that looked very realistic. Greek sculpture inspired artists in later civilisations in many places.

The Greeks also developed special styles of pottery. Red figure pottery developed in Athens in about 520 BCE.

Architecture

The Greeks were very skilled architects. Their public buildings had large roofs supported by rows of columns. The Greek style of building continues to inspire architects today.

The Stoa of Attalos was a covered walkway, built in the second century BCE, in the agora in Athens.

Literature and mathematics

The Ancient Greeks developed their writing from an alphabet used by the Phoenicians. The Greeks first used writing for important matters of government. Later writing included epic poetry and history. A Greek writer called Herodotus is known as 'the father of history'.

The Ancient Greeks made great advances in mathematics, particularly in geometry. The ideas of the Ancient Greek mathematicians formed the building blocks for all future mathematicians and scientists.

Activities

1. Make a list of some historical evidence that tells archeologists about Ancient Greek trade.
2. Work in a group to research the achievements of an important person from Ancient Greece such as Herodotus, Homer, Aristotle, Plato, Socrates or Pythagoras.

Challenge

Use books and the Internet to find out more about the agora and stoa of Ancient Greece. Write about the similarities and differences between these places and modern shopping centres.

2 Review

Answer these questions in your notebook.

Choose the best answer from the choices below. Write a, b or c as your answer.

1. The earliest Greek civilisation was the ___ civilisation.
   a. Mycenaean
   b. Minoan
   c. Phoenician
2. Democracy is an idea that started in:
   a. Sparta
   b. Corinth
   c. Athens
3. The Ancient Greek market place was called the:
   a. agora
   b. stadium
   c. gymnasium
4. The Ancient Greeks liked to discuss ideas about knowledge, truth and the meaning of life. These ideas are known as:
   a. philately
   b. philosophy
   c. philanthropy
5. The rooms in a house that only the men used were called the:
   a. gynaikon
   b. andron
   c. stoa
6. Greek soldiers fought battles in a formation called a:
   a. cohort
   b. cavalry
   c. phalanx
7. The largest Ancient Greek fighting ship was called a:
   a. corbita
   b. trireme
   c. galleon
8. The Ancient Greeks and the ___ controlled trade on the Mediterranean Sea.
   a. Phoenicians
   b. Egyptians
   c. Romans
9. Historical literature was invented by 'the father of history'. His name was:
   a. Homer
   b. Hercules
   c. Herodotus

Rewrite these sentences so that they are correct.

10. The Mycenaean civilisation began on the island of Crete.
11. A Greek warship had up to 270 men pulling the oars.

Now complete these tasks.

12 Look at this map. In your notebook, write the names of the important Greek places shown. The first letter of each place is given to help you.

14 This building is the British Museum in London. It was completed in 1852. Write a description of the building. Include:
- how Greek architecture inspired the building
- the names of the parts you can see
- some adjectives to describe the building.

Look at the photo of the Parthenon on page 21 to help you.

13 Write a brief description of a hoplite's armour and weapons and how the army fought.

15 Write your response to this question: 'Why do we remember the Ancient Greeks?'

2 Ancient Greece

31

3 Ancient Rome

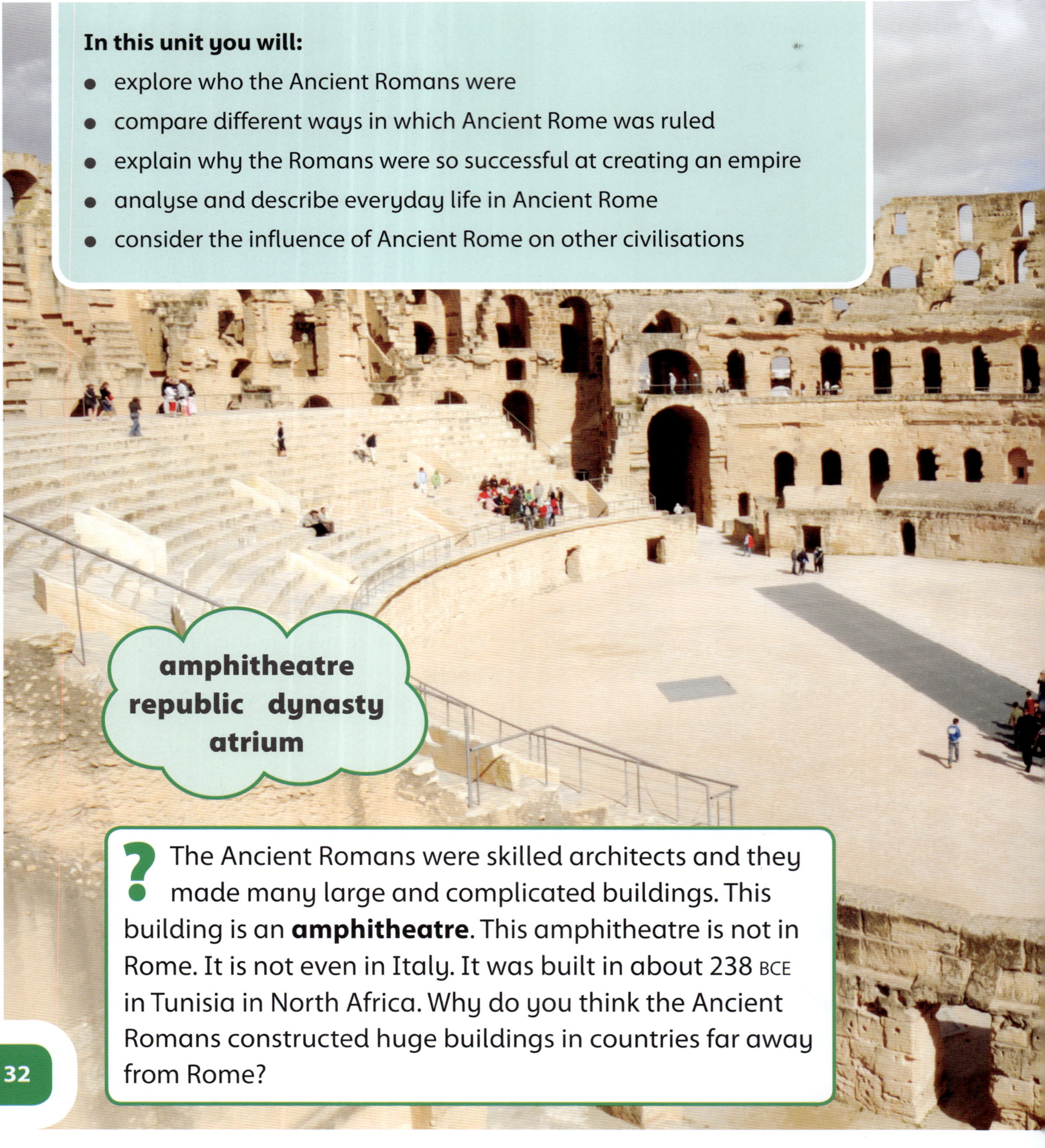

In this unit you will:
- explore who the Ancient Romans were
- compare different ways in which Ancient Rome was ruled
- explain why the Romans were so successful at creating an empire
- analyse and describe everyday life in Ancient Rome
- consider the influence of Ancient Rome on other civilisations

amphitheatre
republic   dynasty
atrium

? The Ancient Romans were skilled architects and they made many large and complicated buildings. This building is an **amphitheatre**. This amphitheatre is not in Rome. It is not even in Italy. It was built in about 238 BCE in Tunisia in North Africa. Why do you think the Ancient Romans constructed huge buildings in countries far away from Rome?

About 2500 years ago, a civilisation developed around the city of Rome in Italy. Starting from this single city, the Romans eventually ruled a large Empire. This empire spread around the Mediterranean and eventually reached from Britain to south-west Asia. The Romans spread their way of life to many different countries. What was the Roman way of life? How did the Roman Empire spread? Why do we remember the Romans?

Ancient Egypt
c3200 BCE–30 BCE

Ancient Greece
c800 BCE–31 BCE

Ancient Rome
509 BCE–476 CE

4000 BCE   0   500 CE

3 Ancient Rome

3.1 The beginnings of Ancient Rome

The civilisation based in Ancient Rome began in about 500 BCE. What was life like before the city of Rome was established? How was society in Rome organised? How were the Romans ruled?

The founding of Rome

The Romans were one tribe of people who lived on the Italian Peninsula. They decided to live together and establish a city. No-one is really sure when this happened, but it is traditional to say that the city of Rome was founded in 753 BCE.

A Roman kingdom

To begin with, the Romans were ruled by kings from the Etruscan tribe who lived in lands nearby. In 509 BCE, the Romans rebelled against these kings. Rome became a **republic**. Instead of having one ruler, the people started to elect their leaders.

Who were the people of Rome?

Men and women who were not slaves in the Roman Republic were citizens. Citizens were divided into two groups. Patricians came from wealthy families and owned land and property. Common people were called plebeians or 'plebs'.

Slaves were also part of Roman society. They could not be citizens and had no power.

How was the Roman Republic governed?

A government is a group of people who make the rules for a city or country. The government of the Roman Republic had three main parts:

Magistrates and consuls

Magistrates were leaders elected by the people. Every year two of the magistrates were elected to become consuls. The two consuls were in charge of Rome for one year. One consul led the government. The other consul was responsible for the army.

Glossary words

citizen	peninsula
elect	plebeian
founded	Senate
patrician	

Senators

The senators formed a group called the Senate. Senators advised the consuls and approved or rejected laws. Senators decided how to spend public money and advised on Rome's relationships with other countries.

Tribunes and assemblies

The tribunes were a group of citizens who represented the common people of Rome (the plebeians) within the government. The assemblies were made up of plebeians. The assemblies elected officials, such as the tribunes, and voted on laws.

Challenge

The Romans displayed their most important laws on metal tablets called the Twelve Tables. Find out and write down three of these laws.

Activities

1. Why do you think the Roman people rebelled against the Etruscan kings? Write a brief explanation.
2. Draw a simple diagram that explains the three levels of society in the Roman Republic.

This is what the Senate may have looked like. Senators debated important issues. They made speeches to try to convince others about their ideas.

3.2 The Roman Empire begins

Some individuals in the Roman Republic wanted more power for themselves. Who were these people? How did they change the way in which Rome was ruled? Who founded the Roman Empire?

Roman power grows

By 290 BCE, the Romans controlled the whole Italian Peninsula.

Expansion into Sicily brought the Romans into conflict with the Carthaginian Empire. In 146 BCE, after 100 years of competition and three long wars, the Romans beat the Carthaginians. They took control of lands and trade around the Mediterranean.

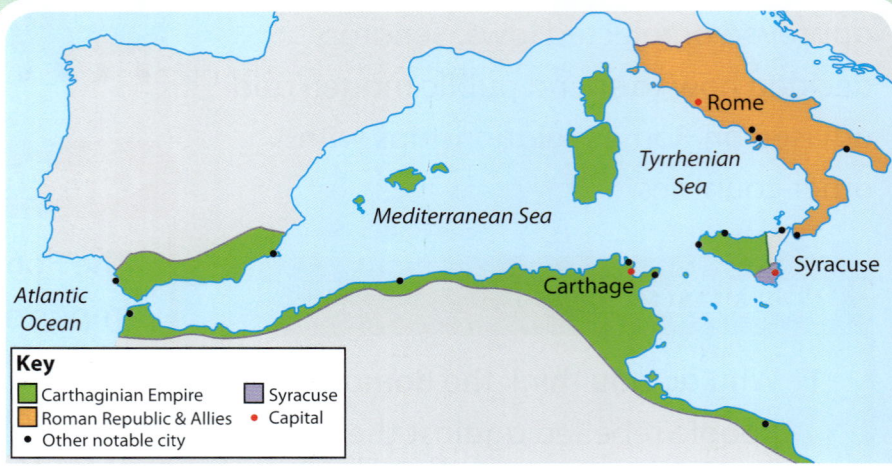

The Carthaginians competed with the Romans for trade across the Mediterranean. Trade was important because it provided resources and wealth.

How did the Roman Empire begin?

Rome was very powerful because of its strong army. The army generals sometimes fought with the Senate.

Julius Caesar was a powerful Roman general. He took control of Rome in 49 BCE. Some senators did not want a king-like ruler and so they killed him in 44 BCE.

Julius Caesar's grand-nephew Octavian later seized power for himself and his name became Caesar Augustus. Augustus ended the Roman Republic and founded the Roman Empire in 27 BCE.

Glossary word

culture

Octavian was the first Roman Emperor and took the name Caesar Augustus. He ruled until his death in 14 CE.

Augustus established a period known as the Pax Romana (which means Roman Peace) that lasted for 200 years. He also established a **dynasty** of rulers. The four emperors who came after him were Tiberius, Caligula, Claudius and Nero.

Why did the Romans expand their empire?

Roman emperors wanted to show their power. The Romans also wanted the valuable resources from the lands they conquered.

People in conquered lands had to pay taxes to Rome. This money helped to pay for the Roman army and for managing the empire.

The orange area shows the Roman Empire in 117 CE.

How far did Roman territories reach?

The Roman Empire was at its largest in 117 CE. The estimated population of the Roman Empire at that time was at least 60 million. This number was about one quarter of the world population at the time. The size of the empire meant that Roman culture had a huge influence across the world. The Roman Empire lasted until 476 CE.

Did you know?

When the Emperor Claudius invaded England in 43 CE, he had a group of war elephants in his army. The Britons had never seen elephants before and were probably terrified!

Activities

1. Write a brief explanation of why the Romans wanted to expand their empire.

2. Work in a group. Find out some facts about the first five emperors of the Roman Empire. Include when they ruled and why they are famous. Make a class poster that brings together all the information.

Challenge

Use books and the Internet to find out about the road network built by the Romans. Write a report of between 100 and 200 words.

3.3 Ancient Roman towns and cities

Cities were centres of activity in Ancient Rome. What was city housing like? Where did people get their drinking water? What did people do for work and pleasure?

What was housing like for different people?

Poorer people lived in two-roomed apartments in blocks called insulae. Each apartment block housed between 30 and 50 people. Insulae were built of mud bricks and timber, and had shops at street level.

Wealthier people lived in private homes. These houses had rooms arranged around an open area called an **atrium**. There were rooms for dining and sleeping and a garden at the rear.

An Ancient Roman street may have looked like this.

How did people in towns and cities get water?

To bring clean water to towns for drinking and washing, Roman engineers developed the aqueduct. Aqueducts carried water to a town from a water source that could be many kilometres away. Aqueducts passed through tunnels under hills and over aqueduct bridges across valleys.

Water went through pipes to different parts of the town or city. Water was available in public fountains and was supplied to some private homes.

The water also carried away waste in sewers.

This Roman aqueduct is in the town of Segovia in Spain. This aqueduct bridge was probably built in about 50 BCE and is 813 metres long.

What work did people do in towns and cities?

Roman towns and cities offered work for many people. Many rich people worked in government. Skilled and educated men worked as lawyers, teachers and engineers. Many people worked as craftspeople making household goods and luxury items for the rich. Towns and cities were full of markets for buying and selling goods.

Slaves worked as household servants or as building labourers.

What types of entertainment were there?

Larger cities in Ancient Rome had a number of buildings for public entertainment.

- There was a circus for chariot racing.
- An amphitheatre was used for gladiator games.
- There was a theatre. Romans liked to watch comedies.
- There were public baths, so people who did not have a bathroom at home could keep clean. People also went to the baths to meet friends.

Chariot racing was very popular. The Circus Maximus in Rome could hold over 150 000 people.

Glossary words

aqueduct
chariot
gladiator
sewers

Did you know?

The Aqua Appia was the first Roman aqueduct. It was built in 312 BCE and covered a distance of 16.4 kilometres from its source to the city of Rome.

Activities

1. Roman towns and cities were laid out in a grid. Work in a group to draw a plan of a Roman town. Show the different buildings and other features mentioned on this page.
2. Work in a group to discuss what life was like in a Roman town or city.

Challenge

Use books and the Internet to find out about the nearest Roman ruins to where you live. Write a report of between 100 and 200 words that describes what archeologists have found there and why the Romans were there.

3.4 Everyday life in the Roman Empire

Family was an important part of life for Ancient Romans. The amount of money that a family had affected many things, from education to clothes and food. What was life like for all the different people in the Roman Empire?

What were families like in Ancient Rome?

The man was the head of the Roman family. Women managed the household, did chores and raised their children. Wealthy women had slaves to help them do these tasks and so they had more leisure time.

Rich children went to school. Education was mostly for boys, but some girls from wealthy families did go to school.

Many girls married when they were young teenagers.

Children of poorer families did not attend school. They had to help the adults in the family with work and daily chores.

What was food like in Ancient Rome?

Most people ate simple foods such as porridge, beans, bread, vegetables, fish and fruit.

At school, children learned reading, writing, mathematics, literature and effective speaking.

Wealthy Romans sometimes invited friends to share food and to enjoy entertainment, for example provided by musicians. Evening banquets often lasted several hours.

Richer people had more variety in their diet and more meat. Their food was often flavoured with exotic spices such as pepper, cloves and nutmeg.

Food varied across the Roman Empire depending on what was available locally.

What did Ancient Romans wear?

Basic clothes were made from linen for the summer and wool for the winter.

Women wore a dress called a stola and a cloak called a palla when they went outside.

Rich women wore jewelled brooches and pins, earrings, rings and necklaces.

Men and women both wore a simple tunic under other clothes.

Richer men wore a toga. This was a large piece of cloth wrapped around the body, with one arm free.

What was it like to live in the country?

Most people across the Roman Empire worked on small farms. A farming family lived in a small house and may have had some slaves to help them.

Rich people owned large estates and lived in villas.

Glossary words

estate   exotic   villa

Slaves and workmen wore a simple tunic made of a rough material.

Important officials wore togas of finer material such as Indian cotton or Chinese silk.

Citizen

Matron

Workman

Slave

Senator

The most common footwear was leather sandals.

Activities

1. Write to invite some friends to an evening banquet. In your invitation, tell your friends what food you will offer and what entertainment there will be.
2. Write a brief description of how life was different for rich and poor people in Ancient Rome. Think about housing, food, education and work.

Challenge

Carry out research and write about all the work done by slaves in Ancient Rome.

3.5 Art and culture of Ancient Rome

The Romans produced art and buildings across the whole of their huge empire. Roman authors produced writings that have been read for thousands of years. What was special about Roman art, architecture and literature?

What can we learn from Roman art?

Roman art included paintings, mosaics and images on pottery. The art often showed scenes from everyday life. Some images were records of important events.

Another popular form of art in Roman times was relief carving. Reliefs are images carved into stone. They are found on buildings and special objects such as a sarcophagus.

The Romans liked sculptures in the Greek style. There were sculptures in homes, places of work, public spaces and public buildings.

What are the features of Roman architecture?

Roman architects used ideas from Ancient Greece, including columns to support large roofs. The Romans developed the arch and also the dome. Arches allowed the Romans to build huge structures including amphitheatres and aqueduct bridges.

Mosaics are large images made of small pieces of coloured glass or stone. Mosaics were used to decorate walls and floors.

This is a small section from the Ludovisi Battle sarcophagus. It was made for an army general in about 250 CE.

Glossary words

arch
dome
philosophy

sarcophagus
sculpture

Roman architecture has inspired architects around the world. Many architects use Roman features in their buildings.

Literature

The Romans wrote in a language called Latin. Important pieces of Roman literature include poems, speeches, histories and works of philosophy.

People continued to use Latin for important documents for centuries after Ancient Roman times. Languages such as English, French and Italian were all influenced by Latin.

This railway station in Washington DC, USA, has arches that were influenced by Roman architecture. The station was completed in 1908 CE.

Activities

1 Work in a group. Prepare a presentation about what Roman art, jewellery and literature tell us about Ancient Roman culture.

2 Work in a group. Discuss what the Ludovisi Battle sarcophagus can tell us about the Roman army and what Romans thought about war.

Challenge

Use the Internet and other sources to find out the history of how domes have been used in architecture throughout the world.

Be a good historian

Good historians know that not all historical documents simply present the facts. Some are written to show events or people in a certain way. What other evidence might a historian use to find out how accurate a document is?

Did you know?

The Pantheon is a building in Rome that is almost 2000 years old. The Pantheon has a dome that measures 43 metres across. A blue whale, which is 30 metres long, would comfortably fit inside!

3 Review

Answer these questions in your notebook.

Choose the best answer from the choices given. Write a, b or c as your answer.

1. Wealthy citizens of Ancient Rome were called:
   a. patricians
   b. plebeians
   c. patriarchs
2. The first emperor of the Roman Empire was:
   a. Julius Caesar
   b. Claudius
   c. Caesar Augustus
3. The Roman Empire reached its greatest extent in:
   a. 117 CE
   b. 14 CE
   c. 44 BCE
4. Insulae were:
   a. public baths
   b. apartment buildings for poorer people
   c. large houses for wealthy citizens
5. The channel bringing water into a Roman town is called:
   a. a viaduct
   b. an amphitheatre
   c. an aqueduct
6. Artists made mosaics by:
   a. painting onto pieces of pottery
   b. painting onto a wall
   c. using small pieces of coloured glass or stone

Now complete these tasks.

7. Look at this map. In your notebook, write the names of the three cities marked. The first letters have been given to help you.

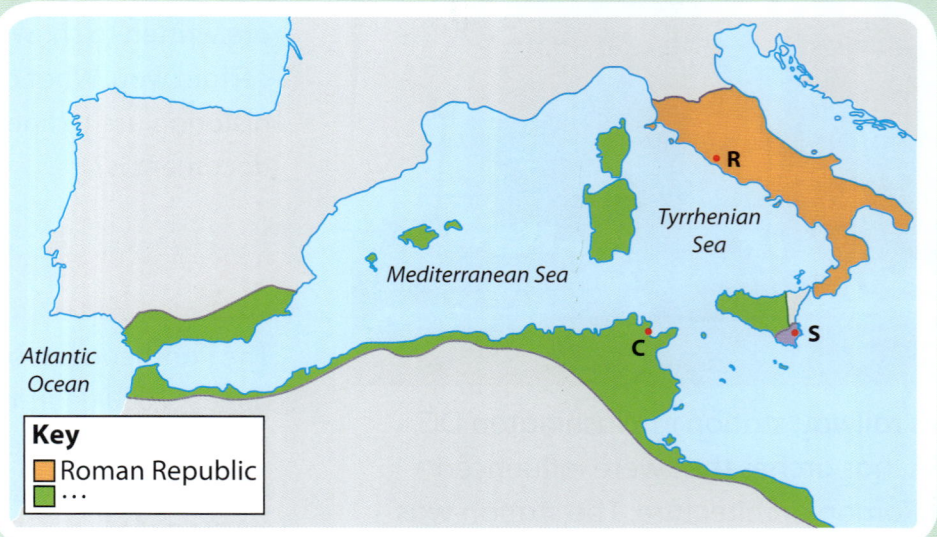

8 In your notebook, complete the key for the map to show who controlled the area shaded green.

Rewrite these two sentences so that they are correct.

9 People and goods travelled between Roman cities along aqueducts.
10 All boys in Ancient Rome went to school.

Look at the timeline that shows the period covered by Ancient Rome.

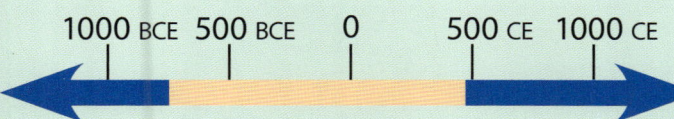

11 Write the name of a civilisation that started before the Ancient Roman civilisation.
12 Write the name of a different civilisation that may have traded with the Ancient Romans.
13 Make a simple timeline that shows the changes in the way the Roman people were ruled over time.

Include the dates for:
- the beginning of Rome
- when the Roman Republic was founded
- when Julius Caesar took power
- when Caesar Augustus became emperor
- the death of Caesar Augustus.

Now answer these questions.

14 The mosaic floor shown below is in a 1st century CE Roman villa in the town of Vaison-la-Romaine in France. What can we learn from this mosaic? Write an archeologist's report describing everything the mosaic tells you. Think about:
- what the image shows
- the technique used to create the mosaic
- the type of people who lived in the villa
- why the villa is in France.

15 'The rulers of the Roman Empire were only interested in using force to conquer new lands.'
Do you agree with this statement?

3 Ancient Rome

45

4 A history of leisure and recreation

In this unit you will:
- explore the terms 'recreation' and 'leisure time'
- identify different forms of recreation over time
- describe ways in which recreation and leisure time have changed
- compare and contrast different forms of recreation over time

3100 BCE Board game called Senet played in Ancient Egypt

1600 BCE Culu, an early form of football, played in the Shang Dynasty in China

530 BCE Oldest known museum

6th century BCE Theatre started in Ancient Greece

100 CE Rich Romans had holidays at the coast and at spa towns

1589 CE First plays of William Shakespeare performed

We spend much of our time doing things we have to do, for example going to work or school, doing household chores, eating and sleeping. When we are not doing these things we have leisure time. In our leisure time we do activities that we enjoy. These activities are called recreation.

Have people always had leisure time? What recreation activities were there in the past? Are recreation activities different today?

board game stadium tournament theatre museum

? What game are the boys in this photo playing? For how many years do you think people have been playing this game? What other activities do people do in their leisure time?

1683	1895	1919	1970s	1990s
World's oldest public museum, the Ashmolean, opened in Oxford, England	First public demonstration of moving picture film	First air passengers travelled between London and Paris	Early computer games	Virtual reality headsets available

4 A history of leisure and recreation

47

4.1 Games

A popular form of recreation is playing games. All games have rules. They also have challenges and a purpose. People have enjoyed playing games for thousands of years. What were the ancient games? How have games changed over time? What is different about the games we play today?

Ancient children's games

A popular game with children in Ancient Greece and Ancient Rome was knucklebones.

Another ancient game was marbles. Archeologists have found clay marbles from the Indus Valley, dating from about 2600–2400 BCE.

Board games

Board games involve moving counters around a special board.

Examples of ancient board games include:

- Senet from Ancient Egypt (about 3100 BCE)
- the Royal Game of Ur (2600–2400 BCE)
- Alquerque or Quirkat from the Middle East (about 1400 BCE)
- Go from China (about 500 BCE)
- Chaturanga from India (about 500 BCE).

The ancient Royal Game of Ur was found in 1928 at an archeological site in modern-day Iraq. Experts believe that this game and Senet were both race games.

Merchants and soldiers helped to spread early games around the world.

In 1892, an ancient Indian game called Gyan Chauper was taken to London, where it became the game of Snakes and Ladders.
In 1896, an Indian game called Pachisi became Ludo in England.

Three popular board games today that developed from ancient games are draughts, chess and backgammon.

A form of chess was played in Persia. People in the Islamic world began playing chess after the Muslim conquest of Persia in 651 CE. Chess reached Western Europe and Russia by the 10th century CE.

This picture is from the 13th century CE. The picture shows a European and a Middle Eastern man playing chess.

People of all ages play chess in countries all around the world.

Many computer games made today use virtual reality. Players use special equipment to interact with computer-generated environments.

Computer games

Computer games and video games first became popular in the 1970s. Video gaming is now a popular form of entertainment and part of modern culture worldwide.

Activities

1. People in ancient civilisations played board games. What does this fact tell us about society and culture in ancient times?
2. Work in a group to discuss traditional children's playground games played in your country.

Glossary words

leisure   recreation

Challenge

Use books and the Internet to research an ancient game. Write a brief fact sheet about your chosen game.

4.2 Sport

People have been taking part in sports since ancient times. What sports were played in ancient times? Why did ancient people like to keep fit and strong? How different are sports and fitness activities today?

Did people play sports in ancient times?

In ancient times, people practised skills for hunting, fishing and fighting. Some of these skills developed into sports.

Ancient art shows activities such as gymnastics, weight-lifting and ball games. These were played from about 1400 BCE in Ancient Mesopotamia, Egypt and in Mesoamerica.

In the Shang Dynasty of China (1600–1046 BCE), soldiers played an ancient version of football. This game was designed to make soldiers stronger – they played with a stone ball!

In Ancient Greece and Rome, sporting activities such as running, swimming, javelin throwing and ball games were popular.

This Ancient Greek **stadium** was built at Messini in Greece in 369 BCE. Crowds gathered to watch athletic events such as running races.

Today, there are major tournaments and competitions in many different sports and athletic activities. These events take place in huge stadiums.

Be a good historian

Good historians see how things from the past develop. People still play some sports from the past today. Some things about these sports have changed over time. Other sports from the past are not played at all today.

How did sports develop?

In Europe, by about 1100 CE, there were **tournaments** for hunting and fighting sports. Tournaments were sporting competitions for rich men involving jousting, sword fighting and horse-riding.

In Japan and China, fighting techniques developed into activities called martial arts. Examples of martial arts include judo, aikido, kendo and karate.

Animal racing with seated riders developed from using animals for hunting and in battle. Archeological evidence shows that horse racing has been popular for thousands of years. Organised horse racing events became popular in Europe in the 14th century.

How did modern sports begin?

Sports need to have agreed rules so that different teams and players can compete against each other. The first 'laws of cricket' were written in 1744 CE. The first rules for modern football, tennis and baseball were all written in the 19th century.

Millions of people take part in sports and fitness activities today as part of recreation. Millions more people enjoy watching sports.

A bat-and-ball game called stool ball

Archery

Skittles

Mob football

In Europe, from the 11th to 14th centuries, sports for the poor were cheap and simple. They included the sports shown in this picture.

Glossary words

jousting   Mesoamerica

Did you know?

In 13th-century England, a law was passed that required all boys older than 7 and all men younger than 60 to have bows and arrows and to practise archery.

Activities

1. Write a brief explanation of how javelin-throwing or archery and rowing may have begun.
2. Write a report for a school newspaper about the history of a well-known sport.

Challenge

Research a traditional game or sport from your country. Find out how it began and how it has developed.

4.3 Have people always gone on holiday?

Holidays are a type of recreation. Holidays usually involve travelling and spending time away from home. When did people start going on holiday? Where did they go and why? How have holidays changed over time?

Early travellers

In order to go on holiday people need certain things – leisure time, money and transport. Most people, for most of history, have not had all these things. As a result, they rarely travelled.

The people who did travel were merchants, royal messengers, pilgrims and soldiers. The history of holidays is closely linked to how time, money and transport have become available to different groups of people.

Ancient holidays

There is evidence that wealthy people in the New Kingdom of Ancient Egypt (about 1500 BCE) travelled for pleasure.

Tourism also existed for wealthy people in Ancient Rome. Special resort towns were built on the coast. Some people even travelled as far as Greece and Egypt.

How has holiday travel changed?

Most forms of transport were first developed to carry goods. Transport includes animal-drawn wagons, ships, boats, barges, motor vehicles, railways and airplanes. All of these were later adapted to carry passengers.

Glossary words

leisure   tourism

Wealthy Romans travelled in a covered carriage called a carruca.

This painting is from 1886. It shows people from Europe visiting the Great Wall of China.

Where did people go on holiday?

People first took holidays for their health. They left the crowded cities to breathe the fresh air at the coast or to bathe in hot springs.

Over time, people also wanted to travel to see sites of natural beauty and historic interest.

Modern mass tourism begins

For many people in Europe, work changed during the 19th and 20th centuries. More people had enough time and money for family outings and holidays. Railways and steam ships created new opportunities for travel in the 19th century. Cruise ships were operating in Europe by the middle of the 19th century. There were three regular cruises to North America by 1896.

There were an estimated 3.6 billion passenger flights worldwide in 2016.

More people owned and drove cars in the 20th century. Airplanes first carried passengers between London and Paris in 1919. By the 1950s, passenger jets were in service. Fast air travel reduced travelling time. Holidays abroad became a possibility for more people.

Mass tourism today

Today people can easily travel around the world. There is a large tourism industry offering many different types of holiday. Countries have natural features and purpose-built facilities that attract tourists.

Activities

1. Make an illustrated timeline that shows how transport used for holidays has changed over time.
2. Work in a group.
   a. Use books and the Internet to find out about the history of tourism in your country.
   b. Write a report that explains how tourism in your country has changed over time.

Challenge

Identify two forms of transport that tourists use to travel to your country. How has people's use of these forms of transport changed over time?

4.4 Storytelling as entertainment

One of the oldest forms of entertainment is storytelling. Stories have helped people understand themselves and their culture for thousands of years. What was storytelling like in ancient times? How have the forms of storytelling changed over time? What has stayed the same?

What was ancient theatre like?

Before the invention of writing, people used storytelling to pass on information and ideas.

Drama and the **theatre** are special forms of storytelling. Theatre began in the 6th century BCE in Ancient Greece.

This theatre was built in Epidaurus in Greece in the 4th century BCE. The theatre had seats for up to 14 000 people. The natural landscape behind the stage area was considered part of the theatre.

Glossary words
opera
shadow puppet
travelling players

Theatre was also popular across the Roman Empire. Theatre developed in China, possibly during the Shang Dynasty (1600–1046 BCE). Traditional theatre in India began between the 2nd century BCE and the 1st century CE.

People have used shadow puppets for storytelling since at least 500 BCE. Shadow puppets were popular in many Asian countries and in the Ottoman Empire from about 1400 CE.

Opera became an important part of Chinese theatre in the 1300s CE and in Europe in the late 1500s.

How did theatre develop?

Theatre in Europe developed from groups of travelling players. They visited market towns and performed in town halls and country houses.

The 16th and 17th centuries were an important time for theatre in Europe. Famous play writers, such as William Shakespeare, worked at this time. Permanent theatres were built in countries around the world.

A flag flying from the pole meant there was a performance.

Actors performed on the main stage.

Richer people sat in the galleries.

New theatres were built in the late 16th and early 17th centuries in Europe.

Poorer people stood to watch the play from this area, called 'the pit'.

Theatre became increasingly important in Europe and America during the 18th and 19th centuries.

Marun al-Naqqash (1817–1855) wrote the first Arabic plays in 1847. A National Theatre was established in Egypt in 1870 by Ya'qub Sanu.

When were films first made?

The first films (movies) were made and shown in the late 1800s. They immediately became a popular form of entertainment.

The first public screening of a film was in Paris in December 1895. Two French brothers, Auguste and Louis Lumière, showed 10 films that each lasted less than 1 minute.

Today there is an important film industry on almost every continent.

Early films were often shown as part of another entertainment such as a fair.

Activities

1. Explain how theatre has been important in different places throughout history. Use information from this page to help you.
2. Work in a group. Research and write about the history of traditional theatre or of film in your country.

Challenge

Carry out extra research into when and where shadow puppets were popular.

4.5 Educational recreation

Many people enjoy visiting an exhibition or a museum to learn about different things. Have people always enjoyed this type of recreation? When were the first museums and exhibitions opened? How have museums and exhibitions changed over time?

Museums and exhibitions

A museum is a building where objects of historical, scientific, artistic or cultural importance are kept and displayed. An exhibition is a presentation and display of a collection of items.

Were there museums in ancient times?

Archeologists believe that the world's oldest museum was built in about 530 BCE in the ancient city of Ur in Ancient Mesopotamia. It is called Ennilgaldi-Nanna's museum because it was built by the princess Ennigaldi. Some archeologists think this was a museum because it contained artefacts from much earlier times, such as clay tablets and part of a statue. The artefacts were neatly arranged and had labels written on clay cylinders. Some of the artefacts were already 1500 years old in Ennigaldi's time.

What are 'cabinets of curiosity'?

In Europe in the 16th century, wealthy families and individuals created private collections of interesting objects. They collected art, rare and curious natural objects and ancient artefacts.

Some of these collections were displayed in 'wonder rooms' or 'cabinets of curiosity'. Some owners donated their collections to create larger museums that were open to the public.

Ole Worm was a Danish collector. He published an illustrated catalogue of the collection from his 'Cabinet of Curiosities' in 1653.

The first public museums helped scientists and historians to increase their knowledge and understanding. They helped ordinary people to learn more about the world.

Are museums important today?

Museums have developed over time. Today, museums use lighting, sound and visual effects. People can interact with exhibits in new ways.

India's oldest museum is the Indian Museum in Kolkata. It opened in 1814 and now has over 1 million artefacts.

Glossary word

artefact

Did you know?

There are now specialist museums for almost every area of life, including: the Museum of Mathematics in New York, USA; the Fragrance Museum in Cologne, Germany; and the Museum of Islamic Art in Doha, Qatar.

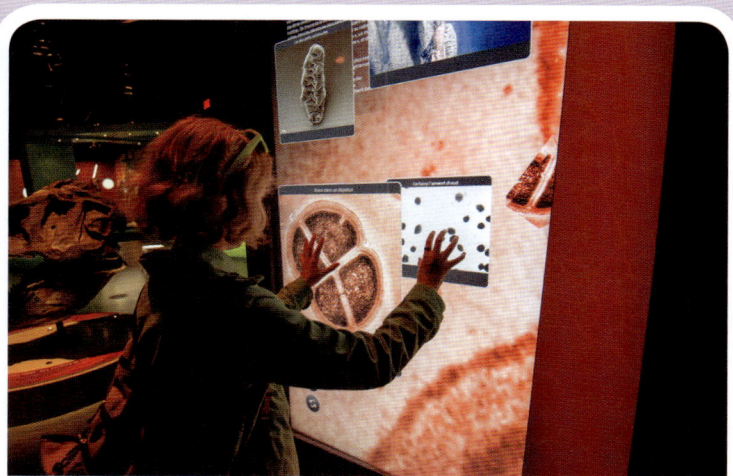

This young girl is using a modern interactive display in a museum.

Activities

1. Write an article for a school magazine that explains why museums are important.
2. Work in a group to discuss different museums near where you live.

Challenge

Carry out some extra research into a museum in another country. Find out when the museum first opened and what it exhibits.

4 Review

Answer these questions in your notebook.

Choose the best answer from the choices given. Write a, b or c as your answer.

1. Senet was a board game played in:
   a. Ancient Rome
   b. Ancient Egypt
   c. Ancient Greece
2. The game of chess came into the Islamic world in:
   a. 651 CE
   b. 720 CE
   c. 1453 CE

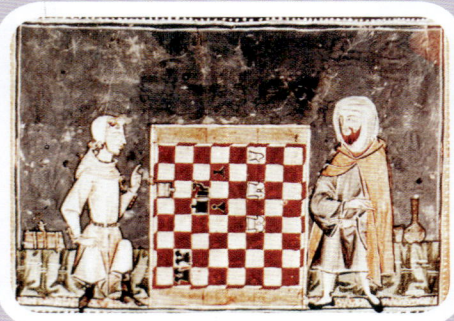

3. People in Ancient Greece watched running races in:
   a. an amphitheatre
   b. a gymnasium
   c. a stadium
4. Mob football was a popular sport among the poor in Europe in the:
   a. 6th century
   b. 14th century
   c. 19th century
5. The first 'laws of cricket' were written in:
   a. 1644
   b. 1744
   c. 1844
6. Holidays became popular in the 20th century mostly because of:
   a. fast air travel
   b. cruise ships
   c. railways
7. Two brothers who made some of the first films were:
   a. Orville and Wilbur Wright
   b. William and Henry James
   c. Auguste and Louis Lumière
8. The world's oldest museum is thought to date back to:
   a. 1530 BCE
   b. 530 BCE
   c. 530 CE

Rewrite these sentences so that they are correct.

9. The first passenger flight between London and Paris flew in 1950.
10. Martial arts such as judo and karate developed in Egypt and Greece.

Now complete these tasks.

11 Describe two similarities and two differences between a theatre in Ancient Greece and a theatre in 17th-century Europe.

12 Think about how people travel for pleasure today and how they travelled for pleasure in Ancient Roman times. Write about some of the changes in the history of travelling for pleasure.

13 Write about two effects that the cabinets of curiosity and early public museums had.

14 Choose one modern sport or fitness activity and one from a period of time in the past that you have studied. Write about the similarities and differences between the activities. Why did people take part in the activity from the past? Why do people take part in the modern activity?

15 Write a short essay about how recreation activities have changed over time. Think about:
- the amount of leisure time that people had
- the types of recreation activities
- people's reasons for doing these activities
- how the activities have changed.

Vocabulary quiz

Answer these questions in your notebook.

1 Ancient Egypt

1 Match the words with the definitions.

   a a large, decorated coffin
   b a person who studies the language, history and culture of Ancient Egypt
   c the group of people who make the rules for how people live in a country
   d the process for preserving bodies used in Ancient Egypt
   e money or goods paid to a government or ruler
   f the person with overall power in Ancient Egypt

> pharaoh   sarcophagus
> mummification   government
> Egyptologist   taxes

2 Write what each of these pictures shows. Then use each word correctly in a sentence or short paragraph.

a    b

c

2 Ancient Greece

1 Which is the odd one out in each group of words? Explain your answers.

   a agora   skyscraper   stoa   theatre
   b gynaikon   andron   bedroom   gymnasium
   c hoplite   cavalry   oarsmen   archers

2 Match the words with the definitions.

   a a play with an unhappy ending
   b a way of thinking about nature, the world and how to live well
   c an Ancient Greek warship
   d a system of government where people are elected to represent the people
   e a person who design buildings and other structures

> trireme   architect   philosophy
> democracy   tragedy

3 Write a definition for each of the following words. Then use each word correctly in a sentence or short paragraph.

   a tyrant
   b culture
   c city-state

3 Ancient Rome

1. Write a definition for the first two words in each list. Then use all three words correctly in a short paragraph about Ancient Rome.

   a patrician   plebeian   citizen
   b dome   arch   architecture
   c fountain   public baths   water
   d consuls   tribunes   government
   e chariot   gladiator   entertainment

2. Sort the words below in a table.

Houses	Entertainment	Government and rulers	Clothes

circus   consul   insulae   emperor
toga   villa   amphitheatre
sandals   tunic   atrium
magistrate   theatre

3. Write what each of these pictures shows. Then use each word correctly in a sentence or short paragraph.

   a

   b

4 A history of leisure and recreation

1. Match the words with the definitions.

   a travelling for pleasure
   b a sporting contest where knights on horseback charged at each another and tried to knock each other off the horse
   c a game in which the players move counters around a special board
   d a building for displaying historical artefacts or other interesting objects
   e a large building with rows of seats for people to watch sporting events

   board game   jousting   stadium
   tourism   museum

2. This is carruca. Explain what it was used for in Ancient Rome. Then write down some newer forms of transport that have been used for the same purpose.

3. Write a definition for each of the following words. Then use each word correctly in a sentence or short paragraph.

   a leisure time   c artefact
   b recreation   d exhibit

Glossary

agora a public open space for holding markets and meetings in Ancient Greek cities

amphitheatre a large building for entertainment and sporting events

andron rooms for the men in an Ancient Greek house

aqueduct a channel built to carry water from one place to another

arch a curved feature in architecture

archer a soldier who shoots with a bow and arrow

architect a person who designs buildings

architecture a style of building, for example Greek architecture

artefact an object made by people in the past

atrium an entrance hall or open court in an Ancient Roman house

board game a game in which the players move counters around a special board

cavalry part of an army with soldiers who rode horses

chariot a two-wheeled vehicle pulled by horses

chores jobs in the house such as cooking, cleaning and washing

citizen a person who has certain rights and responsibilities because he or she lives in a state or country

city-state a city and its surrounding territory that forms a separate state

comedy a funny play that often made fun of rulers and the rich

consul a powerful person chosen from among the magistrates of the Roman Republic

culture the ideas, customs and behaviour of a group of people, shown in everything from language, food and clothing to art, music and literature

democracy a type of government in which the people help to make the rules

dictator in Ancient Rome, a person given absolute power for a short time to deal with emergencies

dome a large rounded ceiling, shaped like half a ball

dynasty a line of rulers who come from the same family

Egyptologist a person who studies the language, history and culture of Ancient Egypt

elect to choose someone, by voting, for a position in the government

estate a property covering a large area, usually containing a luxurious house

evidence things such as artefacts and written documents that tell us about life in the past

exotic unusual and exciting, coming from distant lands
export to send goods to another country
exports goods sold to other countries
fertile land that can produce a large amount of crops
founded established or begun
gladiator a person, often a slave or criminal, who was armed and forced to fight
government the group of people who make the rules for how people have to live in a country
gynaikon rooms for the women in an Ancient Greek house
hierarchy people arranged in groups according to their importance
hieroglyphics a kind of writing from Ancient Egypt in which pictures represented different words, sounds, objects, actions and ideas
hoplite a citizen in Ancient Greece who had to carry out military duties
import to bring to a country from another country
imports goods bought from another country
incense a dried paste of sweet-smelling plant material, burned to release the smell
jousting sporting combat between two knights on horseback – each knight tried to knock the other knight from his horse with a blunt lance

leisure free time
literature written works, such as novels, poems, historical accounts and essays
magistrate an elected official who governed on behalf of the people of the Roman Republic
Mesoamerica a region of Central America occupied by several civilisations before the arrival of Europeans in 1492
museum a building for displaying historical artefacts or other interesting objects
myrrh a sticky, sweet-smelling gum obtained from certain trees
opera a type of drama which has singers who sing all the words instead of actors
papyrus a paper-like material made from the fibres of the papyrus plant
patrician a wealthy citizen within the Roman Republic
peninsula a piece of land that is almost completely surrounded by water
philosophy a way of thinking about nature, the world and how to live well
plebeian one of the common people within the Roman Republic
politics the activities of government
preserve to treat in a way to prevent rotting
pyramid a tomb in Ancient Egypt, built to protect a preserved body and treasure
recreation activities that people enjoy doing in their free time

republic a form of government in which the people elect their leaders, and the leaders are responsible to the people

sarcophagus a large decorated coffin often made from stone, especially used in ancient times

sculptor an artist who produces artwork by shaping materials such as stone or clay

sculpture a piece of art made by carving or shaping material

Senate a group of people who advised the consuls in the Roman Republic

sewers channels, often underground, for carrying away drainage water and waste water

shadow puppet a cut-out figure used to cast a shadow onto a screen

shaduf a device made from a long rod with a bucket at one end and a weight at the other

society all the people living in a country with shared traditions, laws, interests and activities

stadium a large building for sporting events, with rows of seats for people to watch the events

stoa a covered walkway and meeting place in Ancient Greek cities

stonemason a worker who cuts, prepares and builds with stone

tax a payment demanded by rulers or the government

theatre a building for performing plays, with seats for the audience

tomb a special chamber for burying the dead

tourism travelling for pleasure

tournament a sporting competition with several stages and one winner

tragedy a serious play with a message about right and wrong that usually had a sad ending

travelling players a group of actors who toured around giving performances in different places

tribune a person elected to represent the common people

trireme an Ancient Greek fighting ship

tyrant a cruel and unfair ruler who has complete control

villa a large, luxurious house